Moody

By Janine Amos

Illustrated by Gwen Green

CHERRYTREE BOOKS

Moody

First published in 2007 by Cherrytree Books,
a division of the Evans Publishing Group
2A Portman Mansions
Chiltern St
London W1U 6NR

Design. D.R.ink

British Library Cataloguing in Publication Data
Amos, Janine
      Moody – (Good & Bad Series)
      I. Title II. Green, Gwen III. Series
      152.4

ISBN 1 84234 394 7
13 –digit ISBN (from 1 Jan 2007) 978 1 84234 394 4

Maya's story

Maya looked out of the car window. She could see some tents. They must be nearly at the campsite! Maya was excited. She was on holiday with her cousins. It was her first time without her mum and dad.

Maya's Aunty Cass parked the car. Donna, Leroy and Ben swung open the doors. They rushed to the boot and started to unpack.

"Let's play football!" said Ben, bouncing his new ball.

"Let's eat first – I'm starving!" said Leroy.

Donna pulled out her camera. "I'll take a picture of us all," she said. "Smile!"

"Come on, Maya!" called Aunty Cass. "Come and be in the photo!"

Maya ran over and joined in. She gave her biggest smile.

Soon they were all hungry. Ben and Aunty Cass got the picnic ready.

"I've brought something, too," said Maya. She took out the sandwiches her mum had made.

"Thanks!" said Leroy, tucking in.

Maya smiled.

After lunch they went to the beach. It was full of rock pools.

"I've found a crab!" called Maya. Everyone came to look.

"First prize goes to Maya!" laughed Ben. He handed her a piece of wet seaweed.

"Ughh!" giggled Maya.

They played on the beach all afternoon. First they played frisbee. Then they made a sandcastle. Maya and Ben stuck shells round the sides. Donna and Leroy built the moat.

At last Aunty Cass came up.

"That's a great castle," she said. "But it needs a flag." She stuck a feather in the top.

"My mum always does that!" said Maya. Suddenly she missed her mum very much.

It was time to go back to the tent. Aunty Cass held out her hand. "Come along, Maya," she said kindly.

"I don't want to hold hands," grumbled Maya.

Aunty Cass gave Maya a funny look.

At the tent, everyone helped with the barbecue.

"I'm cold!" complained Maya. She watched Donna searching through the rucksacks.

"Has anyone seen the baked beans?" asked Donna.

"That's mine! Now it's all messed up," moaned Maya. And she snatched her rucksack away.

Donna stared at her.

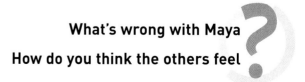

What's wrong with Maya

How do you think the others feel

Ben was sorting out the sleeping-bags.

"Give us a hand!" he said.

He threw Maya her sleeping-bag. But she let it fall on the ground.

"It's all dirty now!" screeched Maya.

"It wasn't my fault!" said Ben.

"You old misery!" said Donna to Maya. "Miserable Maya, that's you!"

Aunty Cass heard it all. "Come on, no arguments!" she said loudly.

"Maya's in a mood!" said Ben and Donna together.

Maya's lip wobbled.

"Come and have a chat," said Aunty Cass quickly, and she helped Maya out of the tent.

"Everything's horrible," sobbed Maya. "The others are calling me names."

Aunty Cass put her arm round Maya.

"They're all mixed up, that's all," she said. "First you were happy. Now you're cross. They don't understand."

"Neither do I," said Maya.

"I expect you're missing your mum," said Aunty Cass. "You're a bit worried about being here without her. It's put you in a bad mood."

"I can't help it!" sniffed Maya.

"It's OK," said Aunty Cass. "Stay and chat with me. And when you feel better, go back to the others."

Maya felt much better already.

"I like talking to you," she said, squeezing her aunt's hand. "It's a bit like talking to my mum."

How did Aunty Cass help

Feeling like Maya

Maya was happy at the beach. She got on well with Donna, Leroy and Ben. Then she began to miss her mum. It put her in a bad mood. And suddenly everything seemed to upset her. She started to moan.

All mixed up

Changing from one mood to another can be confusing. First you're happy, then you're sad. And sometimes it's hard to understand why. The mood just takes you over. It's hard for other people, too. They don't like it. Moaners spoil everyone's fun.

Being moody

If your moods are a problem, you can do something about it. Remember that no one is cheerful all of the time. It's OK to feel bad sometimes. But moaning doesn't help. Talking does.

Think about it

Read the stories in this book. Think about the people in them. Do you feel like them sometimes? Next time a mood takes you by surprise, think what you'll do. Who will you talk to?

Jason's story

"Put that light out, Jason!" called Jason's dad for the third time. It was very late. But Jason still hadn't finished reading.

"OK Dad!" Jason answered. He switched off his lamp. Then, very quietly, he slipped out of bed. He crept to his cupboard and opened a drawer. Jason found his torch and hurried back to bed.

Jason was sleepy. He had school tomorrow. He knew he should put his book down. But he was right in the middle of a pirate story. Jason clicked on his torch. He snuggled down under the duvet and quickly turned another page.

Jason read on and on.

The next day Jason didn't hear his alarm.

"Wake up!" called Jason's mum loudly.

"Mmmm!" went Jason from under his duvet.

Jason didn't have time for breakfast. He ran all the way to school. But he was still late. Jason was in a bad mood.

All morning Jason yawned. It was hot in the classroom. And his eyes kept closing.

"Wake up!" said Jason's friend Sam, giggling.

But Jason didn't think it was funny.

After lunch, Jason's class did their project. Jason and Sam were working together. They were making a book. It was all about the rainforest.

"You draw the snake – and I'll do the parrot," said Sam.

Jason sighed. He didn't want to do anything. He scribbled round and round on the paper.

"Hey! You're spoiling it!" said Sam.

"Shut up!" snapped Jason. He threw down his pencil.

How do you think Sam feels

At last it was home time. Jason's friends were going to the park.

"Let's have a kick around!" said Charlie. He headed the ball to Jason.

Jason missed the ball. But he didn't go after it. He couldn't be bothered.

"What's the matter?" asked Charlie.

"He's in a bad mood," said Sam.

Sam and the others ran into the park. They didn't wait for Jason, and Jason didn't feel like catching up. He wanted to go home.

At home, Jason kicked off his shoes. His little brother Tom was waiting for him.

"Come and play with me!" said Tom.

"Get lost!" said Jason.

Tom ran out of the room. Jason could hear him crying in the kitchen.

Just then, Jason's mum came in. She was frowning.

"Why were you nasty to Tom?" she asked.

"I've had a bad day," said Jason. "I'm in a bad mood."

"That's not Tom's fault," said Jason's mum.

At bedtime, Jason's dad came for a chat.

"I've heard about your bad mood," he said.

"Today's been awful," said Jason. "I've been cross with everyone."

"Do you know why?" asked his dad.

"Because I'm tired," said Jason. "I'm too tired to be friendly."

Do you know what Jason means

Have you ever felt like Jason

Jason gave a big sigh. "Sam went off – and I made Tom cry," he said. "Everyone hates me now!"

"They don't!" smiled his dad. "But I can think of two things to help. The first is to tell everyone you're sorry."

Jason nodded. He wriggled down in the bed.

"And the second is – to get some early nights," said his dad.

But Jason was already fast asleep.

Feeling like Jason

Do you like to stay up late, like Jason? Do you keep getting told to put out the light? It might seem that adults are spoiling your fun. But rest is important for everyone. Tiredness makes us snappy. It can put us in a bad mood. It can make us cross with our friends.

Think of others

What puts you in a bad mood? You may be tired, like Jason, worried or unwell. Whatever the reason, remember how other people feel. They may be hurt if you are nasty to them. Your bad mood isn't their fault. Try to say sorry to the people you've hurt. Then try talking about your feelings. Tell an adult you trust.

Beth's story

Beth was happy. It was the first sunny day for ages. She was going to the city farm with her mum.

"Do you think there'll be lambs yet?" asked Beth.

"I expect so," said Beth's mum. "Now, wear your warm coat – it's still cold outside."

Beth found her scarf and gloves. Then she put on her heavy boots. She hummed a tune to herself. Beth loved the farm at this time of year. There might even be a newborn calf.

It was a long way to the farm. Beth's mum walked fast, but Beth went running on ahead. She couldn't wait.

"Hold on!" laughed Beth's mum. "We must stop at the shops first. I need to get a few things."

Beth wasn't expecting that.

Beth hated going to the shops. This big supermarket was worst of all. The lights were too bright. And the music was awful! Beth followed her mum around slowly.

"Let's do this on the way home," moaned Beth.

"We won't feel like it then," said her mum.

"I don't feel like it now," said Beth.

There was a long queue at the checkout. Beth pulled off her scarf. "I'm boiling," she grumbled.

Outside, Beth's mum saw a friend.

"Not now!" wailed Beth. But Beth's mum was saying hello.

Beth waited. She stood on one foot, then on the other. She picked at a hole in her glove.

Beth's mum didn't talk for long. Soon she called out, "City Farm, here we come!"

But Beth didn't smile.

How do you think Beth is feeling

At last, Beth and her mum reached the farm. It was very noisy. There were ducks quacking and geese hissing. A big cockerel shouted, "Cock-a-doodle-doo!"

"He's saying Good Morning!" laughed Beth's mum. But Beth only frowned.

Then they heard some squeals.

"Look, Beth – piglets!" called her mum.

But Beth wouldn't look. And she wouldn't say a word.

What's the matter with Beth?

There was a crowd of children in the barn. And lots of woolly lambs. "We're feeding the lambs," called the farmer. "Come and join in!"

Beth turned away. A little girl held out a bottle of milk. Beth saw a lamb suck at it hard.

"Ooh! He's greedy!" giggled the girl.

Beth stood in the corner of the barn. She pushed her hands deep into her pockets. She pretended she wasn't watching.

Beth's mum came over. Beth wouldn't look at her.

"Let's go and see the goats!" said Beth's mum. "Or would you like lunch?" Beth sighed and shrugged.

"I'm fed up with this!" said Beth's mum crossly. "We might as well go home!"

"OK," said Beth, pretending she didn't care.

Do you think Beth really wants to go home

How do you think her mum feels

At home, Beth went to her room. She tried to read a book, but she kept thinking about the farm. Beth felt sad.

After a while, Beth's mum came in.

"Have you finished sulking yet?" asked Beth's mum.

"Yes," said Beth quietly. "I'm sorry."

"I know you didn't like shopping," her mum went on. "But we all have to do things we don't like sometimes. And sulking doesn't help, does it?"

"It spoils everything!" said Beth.

Is Beth's mum right?

Beth's mum sat down next to her.

"I wanted to feed the lambs really," said Beth. "I didn't really want to be left out."

"I know," said her mum. She put her arm round Beth. "Shall we go to the farm again next week?"

"Yes, please!" said Beth. "I promise I won't get in a bad mood."

"OK," smiled her mum. "And if we need to go shopping, I promise I'll warn you first!"

"OK," said Beth, laughing.

Feeling like Beth

Have you ever been moody, like Beth? Have you ever felt sorry for yourself and sulked? When you're sulking, you want others to feel sorry for you, too. The trouble is, it only drives them away or makes them cross.

Stopping sulks

Once a sulk starts, it quickly grows. It soon becomes hard to think of anything else. And, as Beth found out, sulking can spoil things. If you're feeling sulky, try not to let the feelings grow. Try to think of all the ways in which you are lucky. Remember, the longer you sulk the more you'll be missing out.

Managing moods

It's hard to cope with moods, even when you're an adult. But bad moods can spoil your own fun and other people's. Learning to manage your moods is part of growing up. And it does get easier – with practice.

Thinking about moods

Think about the stories in this book. Maya moaned, Jason snapped and Beth sulked. And they each learnt something about their moods. What have you learnt about moods – and about managing them?

If you are feeling frightened or unhappy, don't keep it to yourself. Talk to an adult you can trust, like a parent or a teacher. If you feel really alone, you could telephone or write to one of these offices. Remember, there is always someone who can help.

Childline

Freephone 0800 1111

Address: Freepost 1111, London N1 0BR

www.childline.org.uk

Childline for children in care

Freephone 0800 884444 (6 - 10pm)

NSPCC Child Protection Line

Freephone 0808 8005000

www.nspcc.org.uk

The Samaritans

08457 909090

www.samaritans.org.uk